Checkpoint Charlie (2012)

THE BERLIN WALL 1961-1989 *by Ingolf Wernicke*

Construction

World War Two ended for Germany with its surrender in 1945. As agreed by the four victorious allies, the German capital Berlin was divided into four parts: The American, British, French and Soviet sectors. October 1946, saw the first – and at the same time last – free district and magistrate elections for the entire city.

In 1948, after the allies instituted a currency reform in the western sectors, the Soviets blockaded all land and water traffic – including the delivery of food and coal – to the western districts of the city. In November, Berlin was further divided when the Soviet sector was reorganised under a new magistrate headed by Friedrich Ebert (1894-1979). That was followed by the election of a new magistrate in the west, headed by Ernst Reuter (1889-1953).

In October, 1949, East Berlin was made capital of the newly founded German Democratic Republic. West Berlin voted on a constitution in 1950.

On June 17th, 1953, thousands in East Berlin took to the streets and were calling for the end of the SED regime. Soviet troops opened fire on the demonstrators. With the support of the western Allies West Berlin resisted Nikita Khrushchev's ultimatum to "declare West Berlin a sovereign city" and for allied troops to withdraw from the city within six months in 1958.

On August 12th, 1961, the ministerial council of the GDR announced, "To stop offensive activities by revisionist and militaristic powers in West Germany and West Berlin, the German Democratic Republic will institute such controls at its border, including the border to the western sectors of Greater Berlin, as is usual at the frontiers of all sovereign states."

In the early hours of Sunday, August 13th, 1961, temporary fortifications were erected at the western sector boundaries. Roads leading to the west were torn up. The East German People's Army, Border Police and armed factory militias stopped all traffic to and from the Soviet sector.

Under the watchful eye of border troops, East German construction workers put up first barbed wire and, in the days following, a wall made of large concrete blocks. In some areas – for example Bernauer Strasse, between the eastern Mitte district and the western district of Wedding, where the façades of apartment buildings were in the east, and the sidewalks in front were in the west – East German authorities bricked up the front entrances and windows on the lower floors. In this way the walls of the houses were integrated into the frontier fortifications. Residents could only enter and leave by the rear, which was in the east. The first of numerous forced evacuations occurred in 1961 – not only in Bernauer Strasse, but also at many other points on the border.

June 17th, 1953: Soviet tanks at Leipziger Platz

In a television address on August 18th, 1961, Walter Ulbricht, head of the GDR's state council, announced the construction of an "Anti-fascist Protective Wall" (which was the SED's official nomenclature for the Wall) as a measure to "secure peace". In reality, the East German leadership built the Wall to stem the flow of refugees. From 1949 to 1960, some 2.46 million people had fled from east to west, many of them to West Berlin. Some 30,400 people fled in July, 1961 alone. Immediately after the Wall was built, West Berliners were not allowed to visit East Berlin or East Germany.

Berlin's dissection cut 8 S-Bahn (commuter train) lines and 4 U-Bahn (subway lines). In East Berlin, 13 of the 33 U-Bahn stations were closed. The sector and zonal border ran through 193 streets cutting off 62 roads between West and East Berlin.

From north to south, the Wall and border fortifications separated the following districts: Reinickendorf (West) from Pankow (East); Wedding (West) from Pankow, Prenzlauer Berg, Mitte (East); Tiergarten (West) from Mitte (East); Kreuzberg (West) from Mitte, Friedrichshain, Treptow (East); Neukölln (West) from Treptow (East).

In 1962 Berlin had an area of 883.8 square kilometres with a total of 3,279,759 inhabitants. In West Berlin, which covered 54.4 % of the total area (481 square kilometres), there were 2,207,984 inhabitants; East Berlin, which covered 45.6 % of the area (402.8 square kilometres), had a population of 1,071,775.

Border crossings, border fortifications and escape attempts

The fortified border between the GDR and West Berlin around the outer boundaries of the six districts of Reinickendorf, Spandau, Zehlendorf, Steglitz, Tempelhof and Neukölln had a total length of 114.6 kilometres.

Of the 81 crossing points on the sector boundaries between West and East Berlin, 69 were closed immediately on 13th August 1961, and a further five were closed before the end of the month.

That means that only the following seven crossing points remained between West and East Berlin:

Friedrichstrasse ("Checkpoint Charlie") between the districts of Kreuzberg (West) and Mitte (East).

The crossing point Friedrichstrasse was exclusively reserved for the Allied forces, members of the diplomatic corps and foreign visitors.

Bornholmer Strasse between Wedding (West) and Prenzlauer Berg (East);

October 28th, 1961: Soviet tanks at Friedrichstrasse sector boundary

Bernauer Strasse: Bricked up facades (1980)

Wall at Heidelberger Strasse between Neukölln and Treptow (1981)

Heinrich-Heine-Strasse between Kreuzberg (West) and Mitte (East).
Bornholmer Strasse and Heinrich-Heine-Strasse were designated for citizens of West Germany, and at the same time as a crossing point for the flow of goods between West and East Berlin and the GDR. After the permanent visiting arrangements which came into force in 1972, the Bornholmer Strasse crossing point could also be used by citizens of Berlin.
Chausseestrasse between Wedding (West) and Mitte (East);
Invalidenstrasse between Tiergarten (West) and Mitte (East);
Oberbaumbrücke between Kreuzberg (West) and Friedrichshain (East);
Sonnenallee between Neukölln (West) and Treptow (East).
These crossing points were designated for citizens of West Berlin.
The crossing point in Friedrichstrasse station was only accessible to travellers on the S-Bahn (urban railway) and, from 1964, the U-Bahn (underground railway).
In 1961/62, the border barriers consisted of a total of about 12 kilometres of concrete wall. The 7200 cubic metres of concrete panels used to build this wall would have been enough to build 150 single family houses. In addition, there were 137 kilometres of barbed wire barriers with about 8000 to 10,000 kilometres of barbed wire and cleared border strips of about 500,000 square metres with death strips, guard roads and control strips.
In the period immediately after 13th August 1961, 116 guard towers were erected around West Berlin, including 32 towers on the inner city border.
From October 1964 to 1970, the fortifications were expanded into a "modern border". The entire system of fortifications had a length of 165.7 kilometres and ran 50 meters deep.
The Wall was constructed of the following elements:
1. Concrete wall topped by a pipe (3.50 to 4.20 meters tall) or a metal fence (3 to 4 meters tall);
2. Control strip – 6 to 15 meter wide sand strip to ease tracking;

3. Vehicle obstacle – 3 to 5 meter wide pit or tank traps;
4. Floodlights – 5 meter tall lamp-posts;
5. Border guard demarcation - coloured symbols which East German guards were not allowed to pass;
6. Guard road – 3 to 4 meter wide path for motorised patrols;
7. Sensor fence – 2 meter tall fence equipped with sensors that activated visual or acoustic alarms when disturbed;
8. Rear fence – 2 meter tall chain-link fence;
9. Border fortifications consisting of guard towers, bunkers, dog runs, and signalling apparatus between the guard road and rear fence.

In the summer of 1989, the East German fortifications encircling West Berlin amounted to a total length of 155 kilometres, 106 kilometres of which were concrete wall topped by pipes. 66.5 kilometres consisted of metal fencing. The fortifications included 302 guard towers, 20 bunkers and 259 dog runs.

East German border guards were ordered to open fire in case of any escape. From 13th August 1961 to 9th November 1989 there were a total of 265 people killed in connection with escape attempts on the border through Germany, including well over 100 deaths at the Wall in Berlin (statistics:

Chausseestrasse border crossing in the Wedding district (1966)

Sketch of border fortification

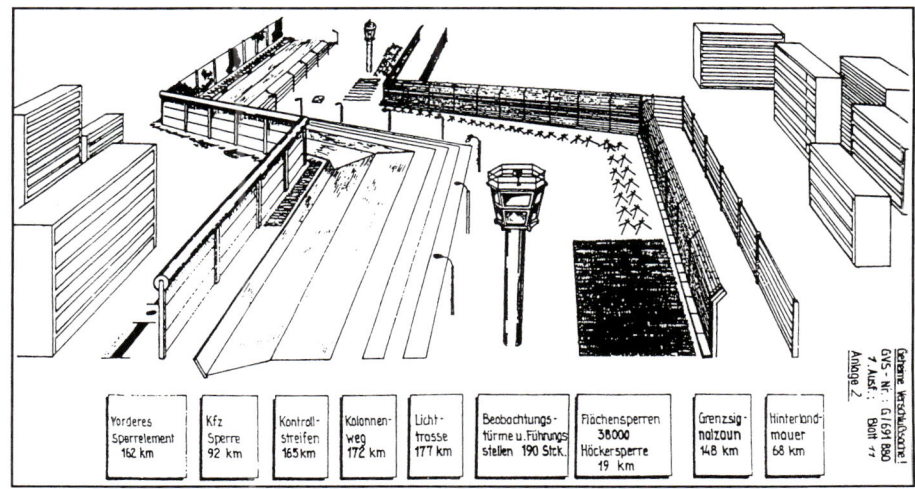

October 5th, 1964: Exit of the tunnel in Bernauer Strasse through which 57 people escaped to West Berlin

trying to climb out of his apartment on the eastern side of Bernauer Strasse. On October 4th, 1961, West Berlin police were involved in a fire-fight with East German People's Police who were on the roof of building number 44 trying to prevent an escape. Under a hail of bullets, 22-year-old Bernd Lünser jumped from a fourth-floor window and died when he missed the sheet held out for him.

On August 17th, 1962, 18-year-old Peter Fechter died right behind the Wall in Zimmerstrasse facing Kreuzberg. He and a colleague tried to flee together. While his colleague reached safety, Peter Fechter bled to death after being shot multiple times in the stomach and lungs. He lay on the ground without aid for 50 minutes, in an area inaccessible from the west, before East German border troops carried him off.

In the first years, many escape attempts were made with specially prepared cars. In 1965, border guards began inspecting motor vehicles using measuring equipment to determine whether or not vehicles were modified.

A spectacular escape by 57 people took place in Bernauer Strasse in 1962. They dug a 145 meter long tunnel 12 meters under the Wall. The tunnel entrance was in Strelitzer Strasse in the East, and the exit was in Bernauer Strasse. However, during this escape there was a gun battle in which the GDR policeman Egon Schulz died.

On July 28th, 1965, the Holzapfel family also made a dramatic escape. They used a home-built chair lift and a steel cable suspended from the roof of the House of Ministries.

Spectacular escapes weren't limited to Berlin. In 1968, a man escaped across the Baltic to Denmark using a mini-submarine powered by a small two-stroke engine. In 1979, two families made headlines when

Senate Justice Administration). 5075 people made it to the west. 574 of those belonged to the armed forces.

Only two days after the Wall was built, the border soldier Conrad Schumann jumped to freedom at the corner of Ruppiner Strasse and Bernauer Strasse. The first victim of the Wall was Rudolf Urban (age 47), who died they used a home-made hot-air balloon to escape from Thuringia in East Germany to Bavaria.

Chris Gueffroy and Winfried Freudenberg were the last two victims at the Berlin Wall. 20-year-old Gueffroy was shot and killed in the Treptow district on February 6th, 1989. Winfried Freudenberg was 18 years old when he crashed his home-made hot-air balloon over the West Berlin district of Zehlendorf on May 8th, 1989.

Border pass regulations and currency exchange rules

After two years of separation between the people in West and East Berlin from 1961 to 1963 and several unsuccessful attempts by the Berlin Senate to negotiate visiting rules, the first visiting permits were granted to citizens of West Berlin in the period from 19th December 1963 to 5th January 1964, and they were used by about 1.2 million people (including repeat visits). In the period up to the middle of 1966, three further border pass regulations were negotiated covering a total of seven visiting periods with different durations.

From 2nd November 1964 onwards, pensioners from East Berlin and the GDR were permitted to enter West Berlin and the Federal Republic to visit relatives.

No other border pass agreements were reached until the conclusion of the so-called "Quadripartite Agreement" in 1971. However, there were border pass arrangements to visit relatives for urgent family affairs such as weddings, births, deaths or serious illness of relatives.

On 3rd June 1972 permanent visiting regulations came into force ("Agreement between the Senate and the government of the GDR concerning the facilitation and improvement of travel and visitor traffic") under which West Berlin citizens and foreigners with a permanent address in West Berlin were permitted to visit East Berlin on 30 days a year (45 days from 1984). At the same time, multiple visit entitlement vouchers were introduced for up to 9 visits in a period of 3 months. In November 1987 the validity was extended to six months, and from 1988 the number of possible visits was increased to ten.

With effect from 1st December 1964, the GDR introduced the so-called minimum currency exchange for visitors. All visitors entering the GDR or East Berlin – with the exception of pensioners and children – now had to exchange an amount of 3 DM (for Berlin citizens) or 5 DM (foreigners and West Germans) at an exchange rate of 1:1. The exchanged money could not be exchanged back, nor could it be taken out of East Berlin or the GDR again. Some West Germans and West Berlin citizens exchanged money at a far better exchange rate in one of the western currency exchange offices in order to make cheap purchases in East Berlin or the GDR. From 1968, all visitors to East Berlin had to pay 5 DM, and visitors to the GDR had to pay 10 DM. In 1973 the mandatory exchange amounts were doubled again, but in the following year they were reduced to 6.50 DM and 13 DM. After 9th October 1980, West Germans and West Berlin citizens visiting East Berlin or the GDR had to exchange 25 DM per day (7.50 DM for young people under age 16) at an exchange rate of 1:1.

The Fall of the Wall on the 9th of November 1989

In 1989, massive floods of refugees from East Germany caused a serious crisis within the Socialist Unity Party's (SED) leadership. On August 8th, 1989, about 100 East Germans entered West Germany's permanent offices (the equivalent of an embassy) in East Berlin, trying to force the East German regime to give them permission to leave the country.

On August 19th, 1989, some 900 East Germans and East Berliners were allowed to cross the Hungarian border into Austria. Thousands of East Germans entered the embassy compounds in Prague and Warsaw. They were given permission to leave after diplomatic support by Poland and Czechoslovakia.

The East German head of state and head of the SED, Erich Honecker, stepped down on October 18th, 1989. On November 4th, 1989, in what was the biggest demonstration East Germany had ever seen, more than 500,000 people gathered on Alexanderplatz calling for democracy and an end to the SED regime.

On the evening of the 9th of November, 1989, the head of the SED's Berlin district and member of the Politburo, Günter Schabowski, announced that, beginning immediately, citizens of the GDR would be allowed to leave the country without complicated formalities. Because of the number of people trying to cross, a captain of the border guards at Bornholmer Strasse gave the order to open the checkpoint completely at about 11.15 p.m. Other checkpoints were also opened.

It was the first time in more than 28 years that the people of East Berlin were allowed to pass freely into West Berlin. The Berlin Wall had fallen.

On October 3rd, 1990, the German Democratic Republic joined the Federal Republic of Germany. Reunification.

November 10th, 1989: Bornholmer Strasse border crossing after the Wall fell

THE "BERLIN WALL" MEMORIAL

Wall Memorial Site in Bernauer Strasse in Wedding (2012)

The central memorial commemorating Berlin's 28-year division is located at Bernauer Strasse. Parts of the Wall and the border fortifications, which have been completely removed almost everywhere, can still be seen here. Integrated into these remains of the Wall is a monument which shows the beholder the reality of the recent German past in an artistically alienated form. Designed by Sven and Claudia Kohlhoff from Stuttgart, the monument was dedicated in August 1998.

The memorial complex can be seen from a viewing platform. The grounds also include the Chapel of Reconciliation and Documentation Center (at the corner of Ackerstrasse) as well as a visitor and information pavilion at the Nordbahnhof S-Bahn station.

The new chapel of the "Versöhnungsgemeinde" (Reconciliation church congregation) was erected in Bernauer Strasse at the site where its original church building was detonated in 1985 because it was directly on the border. The simple building, with a wooden exterior and walls of rammed clay, was designed by the architects Rudolf Reitermann and Peter Sassenroth. Parts of the historical foundations can again be seen, and the altar and bells which were salvaged from the old church also returned to their former site. The chapel building will not only be used for prayer by the congregation, it will also be a sacred setting on the former death strip which will provide a place of contemplation for visitors to the memorial.

And finally, the Documentation Centre shows the 29 year history of the Wall, building alterations and everyday life with the Wall and the numerous events connected with the Wall. One point of emphasis is Bernauer Strasse itself, which was at the centre of the history of the Berlin Wall. A portable Wall Guide is available in the rust-colored information pavilion. The building also offers a good view of the former border strip, where an open-air exhibition on the history of the Bernauer Strasse will open in 2011.

MAP OF THE BORDER

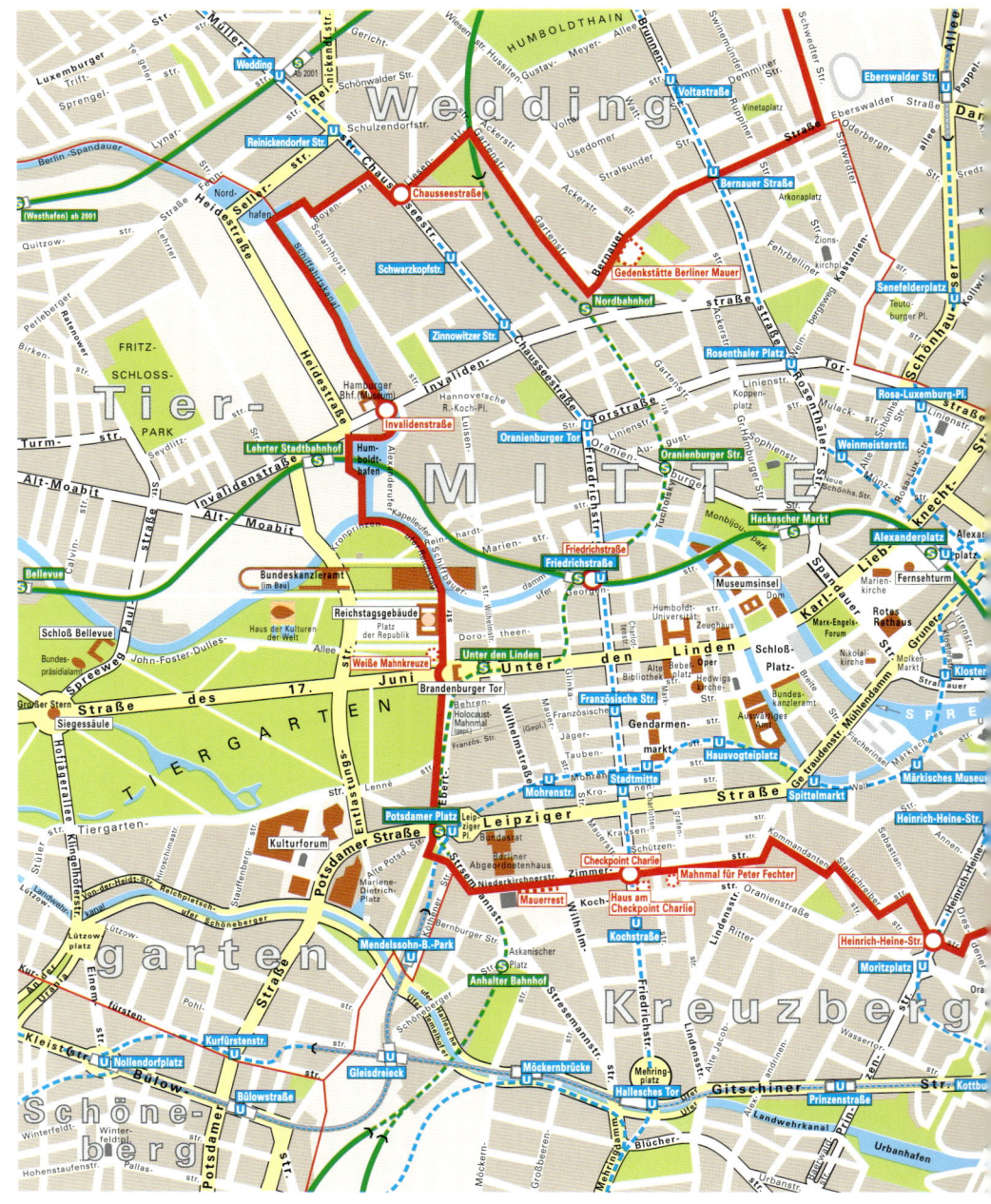

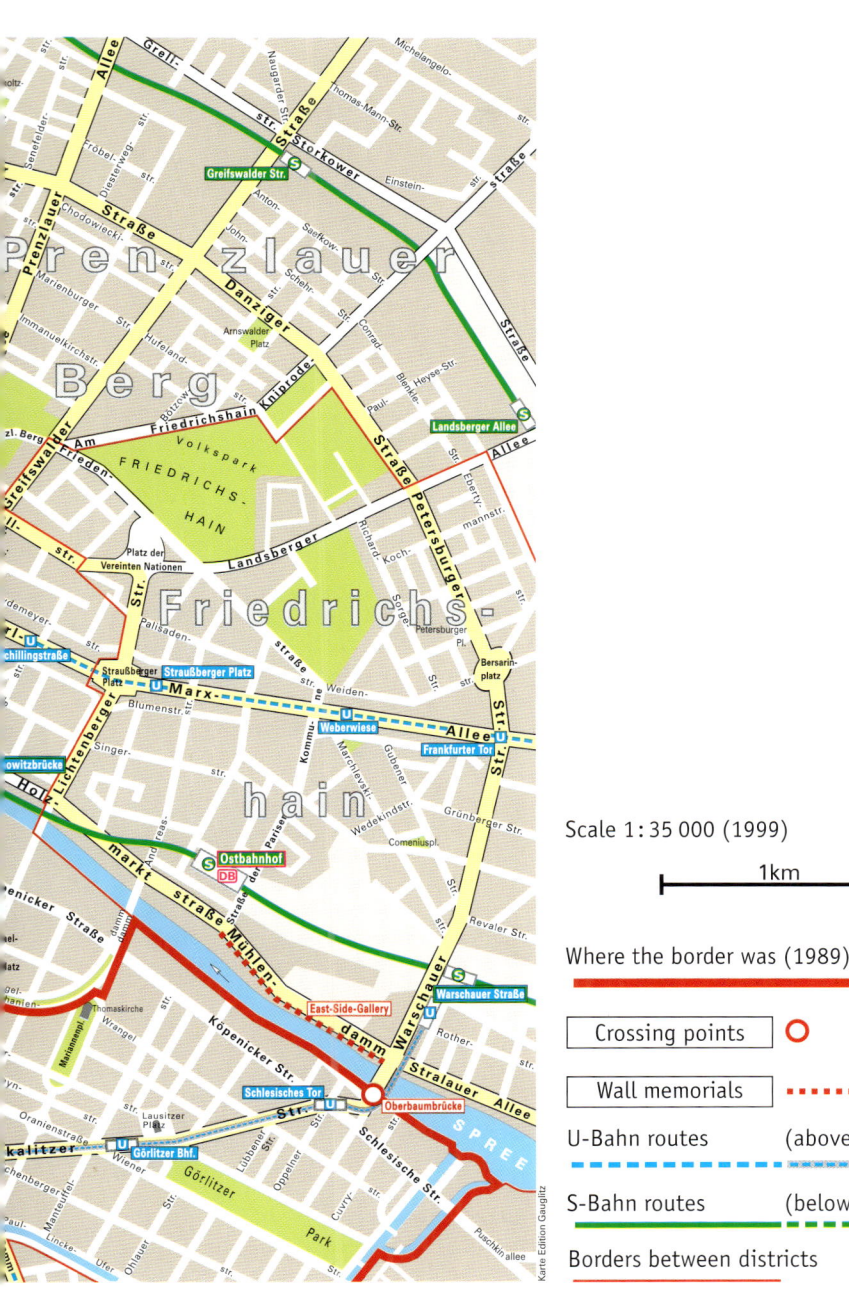

Scale 1:35 000 (1999)

|← 1km →|

Where the border was (1989)

Crossing points ○

Wall memorials ┄┄┄

U-Bahn routes (above ground)

S-Bahn routes (below ground)

Borders between districts

THE WALL – A CHRONOLOGY

13th August 1961
At midnight, troops of the National People's Army begin sealing the border with the western part of Berlin – the sectors of the western powers of France, Britain and the USA – with barbed wire barriers. In the subsequent period the barriers are fortified with solid walls and multiple fences. The corresponding resolutions of the GDR Council of Ministers are announced by radio and television.
Citizens of Berlin on both sides watch the construction of the barriers with shock and horror. In the evening, the Governing Mayor Willy Brandt speaks at a protest rally outside the Berlin parliament: "The Senate of Berlin calls the whole world to witness our accusation against the illegal and inhuman measures of the powers that divide Germany, oppress East Berlin and threaten West Berlin..."

17th August 1961
The three western powers protest in Moscow against the violation of the Four Power status of Berlin.

19th August 1961
Rudolf Urban falls from the window of his apartment while trying to escape – he is the first person to die at the Wall.

19th to 21st August 1961
The American Vice President Lyndon B. Johnson visits Bonn and Berlin. Johnson is accompanied by Lucius D. Clay, the organizer of the Airlift. He underlines the determination of the USA to defend the freedom of West Berlin.

23rd August 1961
The GDR government prohibits citizens of the western part of Berlin from entering East Berlin.

25th October 1961
A face-off between American and Soviet tanks at Checkpoint Charlie after GDR border guards refused to allow members of the US military commission to enter East Berlin. The US personnel had refused to allow the guards to check them because they were entitled to unhindered freedom of movement in the whole of Berlin under Allied law.

17th August 1962
Peter Fechter is shot while attempting to escape and bleeds to death at the foot of the Wall on Zimmerstrasse. The name of the 18 year old then becomes a symbol of the victims killed at the Wall and the inner German border between 1961 and 1989.

23rd to 26th June 1963
With his statement "Ich bin ein Berliner" before an enthusiastic crowd outside Schöneberg town hall during his visit to Berlin, the American president John F. Kennedy underlines the link between the United States of America and Berlin.

17th December 1963
The first border pass arrangements at Christmas 1963 permit visitors from West

John F. Kennedy (26th June 1963)
Speech outside Schöneberg town hall

Two thousand years ago the proudest boast was "Civitas Romanus sum." Today, in the world of freedom, the proudest boast is "Ich bin ein Berliner."

There are many people in the world who really don't understand, or say they don't, what is the great issue between the free world and the Communist world. Let them come to Berlin.

There are some who say that Communism is the way of the future. Let them come to Berlin.

And there are some who say in Europe and elsewhere we can work with the Communists. Let them come to Berlin.

And there are even a few who say that it is true that Communism is an evil system, but it permits us to make economic progress. "Lasst sie nach Berlin kommen."

Freedom has many difficulties and democracy is not perfect, but we have never had to put a wall up to keep our people in, to prevent them from leaving us.

I want to say, on behalf of my countrymen, who live many miles away on the other side of the Atlantic, who are far distant from you, that they take the greatest pride that they have been able to share with you, even from a distance, the story of the last eighteen years. I know of no town, no city, that has been besieged for eighteen years that still lives with the vitality and the force, and the hope and the determination of the city of West Berlin. While the Wall is the most obvious and vivid demonstration of the failures of the Communist system, for all the world to see, we take no satisfaction in it, for it is an offence not only against history but an offence against humanity, separating families, dividing husbands and wives and brothers and sisters, and dividing a people who wish to be joined together.

What is true of this city is true of Germany – real, lasting peace in Europe can never be assured as long as one German out of four is denied the elementary right of free men, and that is to make a free choice. In eighteen years of peace and good faith, this generation of Germans has earned the right to be free, including the right to unite their families and their nation in lasting peace with good will to all people.

You live in a defended island of freedom, but your life is part of the main. So let me ask you, as I close, to lift your eyes beyond the dangers of today to the hopes of tomorrow, beyond the freedom merely of this city of Berlin, or your country of Germany, to the advance of freedom everywhere, beyond the Wall to the day of peace with justice, beyond yourselves and ourselves to all mankind.

Freedom is indivisible, and when one man is enslaved, all are not free. When all are free, then we can look forward to that day when this city will be joined as one – and this country, and this great continent of Europe – in a peaceful and hopeful glow. When that day finally comes, as it will, the people of West Berlin can take sober satisfaction in the fact that they were in the front lines for almost two decades.

All free men, wherever they may live, are citizens of Berlin, and, therefore, as a free man, I take pride in the words: "Ich bin ein Berliner."

Berlin to enter the East again for the first time.

9th September 1964
Pensioners from the GDR can again visit relatives in the Federal Republic and the West of Berlin.

25th November 1964
Citizens of West Germany and West Berlin are forced to exchange a minimum amount into East German currency when they enter the GDR.

3rd June 1972
The "Quadripartite Agreement on Berlin" comes into force and affirms the rights of the Allies in Berlin; the treaty brings a lasting improvement in the living conditions of the people of Berlin. In addition to the easing of travel restrictions to Berlin, the Allies also decide on the exchange of land areas between West Berlin and the GDR. The links between the western part of the city and the Federal Republic are to be preserved and developed. In this treaty, the Soviet Union guarantees free access at any time to West Berlin.

21st December 1972
The basic treaty between the Federal Republic of Germany and the GDR creates the framework for an exchange of permanent representatives.

1st August 1975
The Helsinki Accord is signed, promising easier travel and encouraging more and more people to apply for emigration permits.

13th October 1980
The minimum exchange amount is fixed at a flat rate of 25.- DM.

12th June 1987
In a speech at the 750 year celebrations opposite Brandenburg Gate, the American president Ronald Reagan demands: "Mr. Gorbachev, open this gate. Mr. Gorbachev tear down this wall."

28th October 1987
Separate events are held throughout the year in both halves of the city to celebrate the 750th anniversary of Berlin.

July 1989
From this month, the stream of refugees from the GDR to Austria via Hungary increases dramatically. By 22nd August, the number of refugees who have arrived in Austria rises to 3500.

10th September 1989
Without any agreement with the GDR leadership, the Hungarian government permits 6600 waiting GDR citizens to leave for West Germany without a visa. By the end of September, more than 25,000 GDR citizens emigrate to West Germany via Hungary.
Later, the traditional peace prayers and subsequent demonstrations begin in Leipzig.

30th September 1989
After intensive negotiations between the two German states, embassy refugees – about 5500 people in Prague and Warsaw – are allowed to emigrate.

7th October 1989
Gorbachev visits the celebrations of the anniversary of the founding of the GDR and strongly advocates reforms.

11th October 1989
Leading politicians in the ruling SED communist party admit the necessity of reforms and change, but Socialism is not negotiable.

16th October 1989
In Leipzig, 120,000 demonstrators demand democracy and free elections.

18th October 1989
Erich Honecker, the leader of the ruling SED party, resigns from all state and party positions and is succeeded by Egon Krenz.

4th November 1989
More than 500,000 people demonstrate in the centre of East Berlin. On posters they demand free elections, freedom of travel and democratic reforms. The 26 speakers include the writers Christa Wolf, Stefan Heym and Christoph Hein and the actress Steffi Spira.

7th November 1989
In the evening, the entire government of the GDR resigns without stating any specific reasons.

8th November 1989
The entire "Politbüro" of the SED party resigns; on the same day, the SED central committee elects a new "Politbüro" with the former SED secretary of the Dresden region, Hans Modrow, as the new Minister President.

9th November 1989
At a press conference about the meeting of the SED central committee, Günter Schabowski mentions in an incidental remark that private journeys abroad can be applied for and permits will be issued quickly. Many East Berlin citizens stream to the border crossing points.
In the evening, at about 11:15, the crossing points are opened. The people of Berlin are overjoyed and spend the night celebrating the Fall of the Wall together in the whole of Berlin.

Christa Wolf (8th November 1989)

Dear fellow citizens,

We are all deeply worried. We see the thousands who leave our country every day. We know that misguided policies even in the last few days have strengthened their lack of trust in the renewal of our national community. We are aware of the impotence of words when faced with mass movements, but we have no resource other than our words. Those who leave now reduce our hope. We plead with you, stay in your home, stay with us!
What can we promise you?
Not an easy life, but a useful and interesting one. No fast prosperity, but the chance to help in great changes.
We want to work for
- democratisation;
- free elections;
- the rule of law;
- liberality.

It is obvious that the encrustations of decades have crumbled within weeks. We are only at the beginning of fundamental change in our country. Help us to create a truly democratic Socialism which also preserves the vision of a democratic Socialism – this is not a dream if you join with us to prevent it from being stifled again. We need you. Find confidence in yourself and in those of us who wish to stay here.

Berlin, 8th November 1989

On behalf of the democratic people's initiatives: Bärbel Bohley, "Neues Forum" (New Forum), Erhard Neubert, "Demokratischer Aufbruch" (Democratic Renewal), Uta Forstbauer, "Sozialdemokratische Partei" (Social Democratic Party). Hans Jürgen Fischbeck, "Demokratie Jetzt" (Democracy Now). Gerhard Poppe, "Initiative für Frieden und Menschenrechte" (Initiative for Peace and Human Rights). Christa Wolf. Volker Braun. Ruth Berghaus. Christoph Hein. Prof. Kurt Masur. Ulrich Plenzdorf.

Celebration of German reunification on 3rd October 1990

10th November 1989
At a rally outside Schöneberg town hall Federal Chancellor Helmut Kohl, Governing Mayor Walter Momper, the speaker of the Berlin parliament, Jürgen Wohlrabe and Willy Brandt, the governing mayor at the time when the Wall was built, speak to the people of Berlin. Brandt stresses that he has always believed that the division of the city ran counter to the flow of history.

13th November 1989
Hans Modrow is elected as the new head of government in the GDR by the "Volkskammer". The parliamentary session is stormy. For the first time, representatives of various parties openly criticise the old GDR leadership.

28th November 1989
Federal Chancellor Helmut Kohl presents a 10 point plan in which he advocates the development of confederate structures between the two German states with the goal of creating a federal state structure.

22nd December 1989
Brandenburg Gate is opened in the presence of Federal Chancellor Kohl and the GDR chief of state, Modrow.

24th December 1989
The compulsory currency exchange and visa for West Berlin citizens are abolished.

27th December 1989
A business takes over the sale of segments of the Wall.

31st December 1989
Over half a million people celebrate the New Year at the Brandenburg Gate.

5th May 1990
Beginning of the Two-plus-Four discussions in Bonn between the foreign ministers of the two German states, the USA, Britain, France and the Soviet Union about the external elements of German unity.

12th June 1990
The first joint session of the West Berlin Senate and the East Berlin "Magistrat".

22nd June 1990
Checkpoint Charlie border crossing point is dismantled in the presence of the foreign ministers of the four Allied Powers and the two German states.

30th June 1990
The border regime of the GDR officially comes to an end.

3rd October 1990
Germany is reunified.

ON THE TRAIL OF THE WALL: 8 TOURS *by Christian Bahr*

Even today traces of the wall can be discovered in the townscape of Berlin. Sometimes they are, however, very difficult to recognize, because new buildings and green areas have replaced the former border line at many spots. In any case it is worth to explore testimonies from the time of a divided Berlin on one's own account and to observe thereby how the border, which used to cut through the city, slowly dissolves.

In the following narrative the "Berlin Wall Path" is described in eight tours which cover the most interesting areas of the 155 kilometers where the Wall once stood. The uninterrupted route is accessible to both pedestrians and bikers.

From the Mauerpark to Bornholmer Strasse

The builders of the Wall had an easy time between Prenzlauer Berg and Wedding. Railroad tracks and railroad grounds already formed a "natural" barrier between the neighboring districts. Bit by bit, Berlin gradually transformed the additional grounds of the border into a natural hiking trail. It begins at the Mauerpark, where a piece of the former inner wall on the hill is used by graffiti artists. This popular park at Eberswalder und Schwedter Strasse was created after the city was reunified. In the summer it becomes a place for events, where concerts and festivals can be visited. The Schwedter Steg, a good five hundred meter long path over the railroad grounds, leads to Behmstrasse. The reconstruction of the Behmstrasse Bridge (1994–2001) again connects the districts of Prenzlauer Berg and Wedding – 13 years after the fall of the Wall.

Beneath the Behmstrasse, continue along the Norwegerstrasse towards the Bösebrücke. The "Bornholmer Strasse" border-crossing was located at the Bösebrücke. An inconspicuous commemorative stone recalls the momentous night of November 9, 1989. This is the first place where the Wall opened. Border troops gave in to the pressure of the masses and opened up the turnpikes. On the north edge

Closed S-Bahn station at Bornholmer Strasse (1980)

of the road there is still a piece of the old concrete wall from the border area. Information panels there describe the fall of the Wall and the peaceful revolution in the GDR.

If you leave Bornholmer Strasse again and head towards the garden colony, you can walk along the former death strip. Today Japanese cherry trees align the old border troop patrol path. The trees were donated in December 1993 by citizens of Japan in an expression of joy over the reunification. "Here under the branches of the cherry trees in bloom no-one is foreign" is inscribed on a memorial stone. A stroll along the garden colony is particularly lovely in the springtime.

Or you might consider taking a short trip with the S-Bahn along the former border grounds between Bornholmer Strasse and Wollankstrasse. The route along the border still operated when the city was divided. A storage area had been situated between the two railroad tracks just beyond Bornholmer Strasse. Beginning in 1990, the torn down pieces of the Wall were scrapped and shredded here.

The Wollankstrasse train station was a one-of-a-kind during the time of division. It was situated on eastern territory but used by the West. From the northern exit at Schulzestrasse you can reach the old border strip, positioned between the railway embankment and residential buildings. That is also where the cherry tree lane starts again and continues all the way to the Bürgerpark.

The old border lampposts still exist in part along the grassy strip (but the covers are new). Old electricity boxes can also be found hidden behind overgrown shrubs.

U-Bahn station Eberswalder Strasse or Bernauer Strasse, S-Bahn station Bornholmer Strasse
Time: ca. one hour

August 1961: Escape from the Eastern sector through the window; the pavement in front of the building on Bernauer Strasse belonged to the Western sector

Bernauer Strasse

Nowhere in Berlin were the drastic consequences of the divided city presented to the world more clearly than at Bernauer Strasse. And nowhere can the absurdity of the division be more vividly felt today than at Bernauer Strasse. This is one reason why Berlin erected the Berlin Wall Memorial here on the former border grounds. An exhibition from 2012 provides an in-depth presentation of the historical events that occurred here. The victims of the Berlin Wall are commemorated here too.

If you arrive from the Nordbahnhof station, be aware that you are exiting into former no man's land. The underground station, like 15 other stations, was for 28 years a "ghost station". Closed off and walled up because the West Berlin lines crossed East Berlin territory. From the Bernauer Strasse exit you practically step onto the area where the Wall once stood. And a short way from here stands the actual wall, about 80 meters of it, which was spared from demolition in the summer of 1990.

Before August 13, 1961, the Bernauer Strasse was a normal residential street in a densely populated Berlin neighborhood. On both sides of the street there stood tenement houses, lined up one after the other. None of that remains today. Especially fateful for Bernauer Strasse was, that the street belonged to a borough of the West called Wedding, whereas the houses on the south side were part of the east district of Mitte. The neighbors at Bernauer Strasse lived in different sectors. For the residents of buildings no. 1–50, this meant that after August 13, their windows facing Bernauer Strasse were the border to the GDR. As a matter of course when the border went up, the doors of these buildings were sealed – but not the windows. That came later. So hundreds of people began to flee through the windows. There were dramatic scenes: People desperately slid down the front, jumped from the upper floors, fell into the security nets of the West Berlin fire department. There were deaths. Ida Siekmann jumped from the third floor on August 22, 1961, and missed the mattress that had been put out to catch her fall.

The builders of the Wall put a harsh stop to the "window jumps". In September the residents on the East Berlin side were forced to leave their apartments. The empty apartments were permanently walled up and later torn down. A broad, perfected border strip

January 28th, 1985: Demolition of the church of Reconciliation on the death strip near Bernauer Strasse

1 Gedenkstätte Berliner Mauer
2 Dokumentationszentrum
3 Versöhnungskirche
4 Tunnel 29
5 Mauerpark

was put up in their place and can still be seen today in the middle of the residential area. In order to increase visibility across the grounds, the GDR blew a church up in 1985. For 24 years it stood in the death strip, inaccessible, but heavily symbolic, and that was a thorn in the side of the GDR government. On the grounds of the Reconciliation Church, vis à vis Hussitenstrasse, a new Chapel of Reconciliation has been erected.

When the above ground escape routes were blocked, people began to dig secret tunnels beneath the Bernauer Strasse. At the corner of Wolgaster Strasse, for example, 29 people escaped through the "Tunnel 29". The largest escape tunnel was completed in 1964. It began in the basement of a shut down bakery. It ran twelve meters deep and 145 meters to the east. From October 3–5, 1964, 57 refugees crawled through the narrow passageway to the West. On the third night the tunnel was discovered by GDR border guards.

The memorial's central monument lies at the corner of Ackerstrasse. Based on an idea of Sven and Claudia Kohlhoff, a section of the border grounds has been enclosed by two six meter high steel walls. The death strip here can only be viewed through narrow slits in the original back wall. The viewing platform on top of the Berlin Wall Documentation Center, which is located across the street at Bernauer Strasse 111, provides an expansive view of the border grounds from above. The tour ends at the "Mauerpark" (Wall park) on Eberswalder Strasse.

S-Bahn station Nordbahnhof, U-Bahn station Bernauer Strasse
Time: 45 minutes

Invalidenstrasse

This Wall tour goes from border-crossing to border-crossing.

If you turn right at the former checkpoint Chausseestrasse you will come to Boyenstrasse, that leads to the Spandauer Shipping Canal. This used to be the death strip. The street ends at the Bundeswehr hospital, which used to be part of the GDR government hospital before 1989. Continuing along Scharnhorststrasse, turn into the Kieler Strasse. Just before the canal, between two new residential buildings, you'll find an original watchtower from the former Wall strip.

Inside the tower, a small exhibit commemorates the first victim of the shooting order at the Wall. Günter Litfin was 24 years old when, just 11 days after the border was closed, he was shot by East German policemen as he tried to flee to West Berlin by swimming through the Humboldt Harbor (located at the end of the tour).

After the Wall fell, the strip of the border was transformed into an attractive river-bank promenade. If you follow it to the south you'll come to a green area with a few scattered gravestones. This is the Invaliden Cemetery.

Half of this historically significant cemetery was recklessly leveled when the border was put up. These elaborate graves were destroyed and taken away so that a "fire and observation field" could be established. The SED regime did not have a problem with this desecration of culture and graves, especially since it was primarily officers and generals of the hated Prussian monarchy who were buried here. Three pieces of the Wall have been preserved on the grounds, including a 100 meter long hinterland wall that cuts straight through the cemetery over graves and burial sites. The renovated old cemetery wall on the canal was used as a barrier to the West.

The canal promenade continues behind the Federal Ministry of the Economy. On the opposite side of the canal you can see the Hamburg Station Museum. In May 1962 GDR border guards and West Berlin police officers exchanged fire here. The conflict erupted because the border soldiers continued to recklessly shoot at a 15-year-old refugee, even after he had already reached the safe bank of the West. So the West Berlin police returned the fire. The 21-year-old border soldier, Peter Göring, was fatally injured. Most likely by a ricocheted bullet from his own troops.

The Sandkrug Bridge was built in 1994 where the "Invalidenstrasse" border-crossing used to be.

Traces of the border – walled up building entrances and barred windows – can still be found along Invalidenstrasse.

U-Bahn station Reinickendorfer Strasse,
S-Bahn station Hauptbahnhof
Time: 45 minutes

Reichstag and Brandenburg Gate

After the Wall opened, the Berliners had only one wish: That the Wall that so brutally partitioned the city disappear at once. Berlin did not want an ugly scar in its center any longer. The parliament quarter around the Reichstag and the Pariser Platz illustrate perfectly how Berlin pursued its heartfelt wish. A line of stones paved into the street where the Wall once stood is the only reminder of the division. The new buildings of the Bundestag purposefully connect the two city parts that had once been separated. The Reichstag building used to stand alone with its back to the Wall. The border ran along the east side of the German parliament building. The Spree, too,

View of the Wall in front of Brandenburg Gate from the roof of the Reichstag building (1962)

The Wall and the Brandenburg Gate seen from the west (1980)

had been part of the boundary. Today the parliamentarians work in offices that are situated directly on the former Wall strip.

The Old Palace of the Reichstag president, today the residence of the Parliamentary Society, survived the demolition craze of the GDR government. Next to the Reichstag, it used to stand on border territory and was often used as a listening post by the Stasi.

The plaza between both buildings, today the entrance reserved for politicians, had once been the "death strip". Stone slabs of granite recall where the Wall once ran its course. On the south side of the Reichstag building, at the Tiergarten park, and on the bank of the Spree, white crosses commemorate the

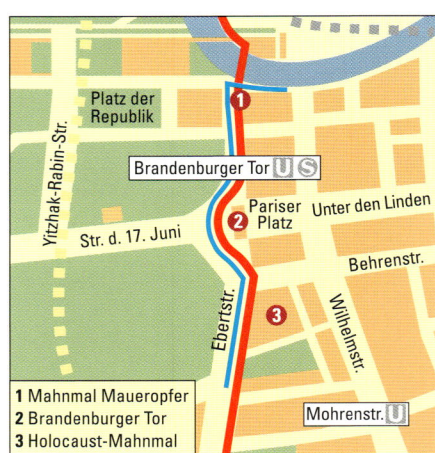

1 Mahnmal Maueropfer
2 Brandenburger Tor
3 Holocaust-Mahnmal

people who lost their lives at the Wall. On the other side of the Spree, north of the Bundestag library, a piece of art by Ben Wargin recalls the division: The "Parliament of Trees" was created from concrete segments of the Wall and partially cuts through the ground level of the Marie Elisabeth Lüders Building.

When the Wall still stood, the Brandenburg Gate was a lonely symbol. Unreachable both from the East and the West, it stood tightly guarded within the grounds of the border. Only state visitors of the GDR were able to visit the historical city gates. From the west side, however, it was possible to come pretty close to the landmark. In the East the barriers stood far back at the Hotel Adlon. The Pariser Platz was completely empty.

The Gate was always a political issue. After the war, the heavily damaged structure was rebuilt in a cooperative effort between East and West. The reproduction of the "Quadriga" was cast by a foundry located in West Berlin. The eagle and Iron Cross in the laurel wreath of the Goddess of Victory, Prussian symbols from the wars of liberation against Napoleon's occupation, had been removed by the leaders of the GDR. After unification and following a long discussion, they were returned.

On December 22, 1989, the GDR minister president Hans Modrow and Federal Chancellor Helmut Kohl opened the Brandenburg Gate to traffic. After the reunification, on October 3, 1990, the gate was tied up into the heavy traffic of the new city center. Since October 3, 2002 all traffic has been banned from Pariser Platz and the Brandenburg Gate.

South of the Berlin landmark the "field of steles" commemorates the victims of the Holocaust. The memorial by the architect Peter Eisenman, completed in 2005, also contains an underground "Place of Information."

*S- and U-Bahn station Brandenburger Tor
Time: 20 minutes*

From Potsdamer Platz to Niederkirchnerstrasse

The Potsdamer Platz, once the heart of Berlin, a world famous business district and pulsating traffic junction, was hurt the worst by the Wall. It was simply buried under walls, anti-tank obstacles and no man's land. And quite rigorously. Ruins in the eastern sector that were left from the war were torn down. The Potsdam train station, Haus Vaterland, Haus Columbus and the Wertheim department store disappeared. The S-Bahn and U-Bahn stations were walled up. In the West, the only buildings that were spared during the reparceling of urban land were the Huth Weinhaus and the remains of the Grand Hotel Esplanade. A cosmopolitan city became a wasteland, a military no man's land in the middle of the city.

Although there was nothing to see there, busloads of tourists always headed for the

In front of the Reichstag: Globetrotter S-Bahn – transit train from East to West

lifeless area. Visitors looked in amazement at the huge expanse of the death strip. The leaders of the GDR rule had been able to destroy the architecture, but not the aura of the area.

It was therefore no surprise that three days after the Wall fell, on November 12, 1989, the GDR removed a large piece of the Wall from Potsdamer Platz and established a new border-crossing there. Starting then, life returned to the plaza. This event is remembered by illustrated segments of the Wall that stand next to the glass office tower at the entrance to the Potsdamer Platz train station. Stone slabs in the ground indicate where the Wall once stood.

Potsdamer Platz, once the intersection of the American, British and Soviet sectors, was also the site where on June 17, 1953, the conflict broke out between demonstrating GDR workers and Soviet tanks.

If you continue south along the Stresemannstrasse, on the left you'll see colorfully painted pieces of the Wall on the ground floor of a ministry building. They are standing at their original location. The narrow Erna-Berger-Strasse leads to a historically protected watchtower. When the Wall still stood, it was only possible to walk on the west side of the Stresemannstrasse sidewalk. Pieces of the Wall were also placed on the lawn of the neighboring Leipziger Platz, marking the historical route.

A very long piece of the Wall has been preserved on Niederkirchnerstrasse, which runs

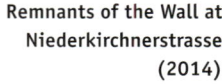

Remnants of the Wall at Niederkirchnerstrasse (2014)

off Stresemannstrasse. This section of the Wall was heavily marred by "Wall-peckers", who after November 9, 1989, attacked the border barrier with their tools. This wall, where today the exhibition "Topography of Terror" is displayed, was the border to the West. Two dark chapters of German history collide here. At an earlier time, the terror apparatus of the Third Reich, the Gestapo and SS headquarters, had been located on these grounds.

The huge building on the other end of the Wall is the seat of the Federal Ministry of Finance. In the GDR it had been the "House of Ministries" and after that, until 1994, it served as the office of the trust company for the privatization of East German businesses. Originally the office complex was built by the Nazis as an Aviation Ministry. An exhibition about the workers' uprising in 1953 was erected on the front plaza on Leipziger Strasse in 2013.

The Berlin Parliament Building (Abgeordnetenhaus) used to be the Prussian State Parliament (Landtag).

S- and U-Bahn station Potsdamer Platz
Time: 30 minutes

The Wall at Potsdamer Platz and the dilapidated S-Bahn stations in the foreground (1965)

October 26th, 1961: American-Soviet confrontation at Checkpoint Charlie

Checkpoint Charlie

Checkpoint Charlie is known throughout the world and is one of Berlin's most popular sightseeing attractions. The former border-crossing between the American sector (Kreuzberg) and the Soviet sector (Mitte) divided the Friedrichstrasse, the central axis of the city center.

The small, white guardhouse of the US army that was rebuilt in 2001 for the 40th anniversary of the building of the Wall, recalls the episode that almost inflamed the Cold War. In October 1961, American and Soviet tanks stood at this intersection just a hundred meters apart in a face off.

The confrontation began on October 22, 1961, when the GDR flexed its muscle. At this crossing, which was only used by members of the Allies and foreigners, the GDR People's Policeman on duty demanded the ID of US envoy, Allan Lightner, before allowing him to enter East Berlin. Lightner furiously refused since according to Berlin's four-power status, only the Soviet army had that authority. After the GDR border officers repeated this game on the following days, the American general, Lucius D. Clay, reacted with the means at his disposal – those of a world power: A number of American tanks moved into position on October 25 at 8:30 a.m. on the west side of Checkpoint Charlie.

1 Mauermuseum
2 Checkpoint Charlie
3 Mahnmal für Peter Fechter

A battle of nerves and endurance began. On October 26 the Soviet sector called in their tanks. The situation became threatening. The confrontation between both world powers could escalate into an armed conflict. The telephone lines between Washington and Moscow were buzzing. After about 48 hours later, the Soviet tanks withdrew. Shortly thereafter, the Americans cleared out their position. The GDR leadership had to give in: Allied officers could once again enter East Berlin unchecked. Neither of the superpowers wanted a war over Berlin. The Soviet leader Nikita Khrushchev explained in short: "If the tanks moved forward, that meant war. If they moved back, that meant peace." The Cold War Black Box on the checkpoint grounds provides a glimpse into the time of the east-west conflict. An information wall with texts

Tourist attraction Checkpoint Charlie (2013)

and photos describes the events surrounding the Iron Curtain that once divided Berlin.

If you walk two blocks east along Zimmerstrasse, which was once the death strip, you'll come across the memorial for Peter Fechter. About a year after the Wall had been put up, on August 17, 1962, the 18-year-old bricklayer apprentice decided to flee with a friend to the West. The two young men climbed over the fence outside the control strip and suddenly came under the fire of the border soldiers. 35 bullets were shot in total. His friend managed to climb over the tall wall in the hail of bullets. Peter Fechter, shot in the stomach and back, laid with his serious wounds on the east side of the wall. No-one came to his assistance as he bled to death. Not the GDR border guards, nor the US soldiers on duty at Checkpoint Charlie. Fechter cried out for help but the policemen from West Berlin, on the other side, were unable to reach him. Hundreds of Berliners listened as the young boy's painful cries became fainter. After about an hour, the lifeless Fechter was carried away by the GDR border policemen. The bronze statue recalls Peter Fechter's agonizing death. He was the 31st fatal victim in the first year of the Wall's existence.

Weeks earlier, on June 18, 1962, the border soldier Reinhold Huhn had been shot and killed by a refugee on the Zimmerstrasse.

U-Bahn station Kochstrasse or Stadtmitte
Time: 30 minutes

Bethaniendamm and Engelbecken

This tour travels along the district border to Kreuzberg, the neighborhood with the highest population density in all Berlin. The building of the Wall had serious consequences for this working-class district which was practically closed off by it on three sides. The border to the Mitte district today, which then also functioned as the sector border, runs along Waldemarstrasse, at the corner of Leuschnerdamm. The gardens in the middle of Leuschnerdamm and Legiendamm are worth taking a closer look at. The green middle strip developed in 1926 along the route of the Luisenstadt Canal that had been filled

Park by the Luisenstadt canal (1928)

hind the border line on eastern territory. As a result there was a narrow strip between the Wall and the western sector that was still under the jurisdiction of the GDR. It was used by border troops to do maintenance work on the Wall or for patrolling. West Berliners also took over this piece of no man's land and planted for instance gardens on it. Such idylls were prohibited by the GDR, but usually tolerated. The Wall turned the Leuschnerdamm into a medieval-like street. All but the sidewalk remained off-limits to the western residents. Today they can once again enjoy the restored gardens. The 22 meter long water-filled "Engelbecken" (angel basin) is especially popular. A number of new buildings were erected on the west side of the grounds.

U-Bahn station Kottbusser Tor
Time: 45 minutes

up after it was no longer in use. The narrow park with imaginative garden ornamentation continued all the way to Köpenicker Strasse. On August 13, 1961, the recreational area was buried under the Wall and anti-tank obstacles. The Wall bordered the sidewalk directly on Leuschnerdamm and around the bend to Bethaniendamm. The sidewalk actually belonged to the eastern sector. Only the houses stood on western territory.

But as in other areas as well, the GDR government situated the barrier a few meters be-

East-Side-Gallery

Along Mühlenstrasse at the Ostbahnhof station in Friedrichshain, East Germans had the rare "pleasure" of seeing the border grounds in a way, which was usually a privilege reserved for westerners. Because the Spree river made up the border here, the GDR government had to erect the concrete wall to the west sector on its own river bank. After the SED regime collapsed, artists from Eastern Europe had the opportunity to paint the now purposeless wall as westerners had done for years. 118 artists from 21 countries immortalized themselves along the 1.3 kilometer long wall. Some politically, others poetically, some ironically, others idealistically. The imaginative work of art captured the atmosphere of the time. The "East-Side-Gallery" is on of the most popular sites in Berlin. In 2009, the artists restored the paintings, some of which have achieved worldwide acclaim.

1 Engelbecken
2 ehemaliger Todesstreifen

30

If you start from the Ostbahnhof and walk along the "East-Side-Gallery", you'll come to the Oberbaum Bridge. The neo-Romanesque structure is the longest of all historical bridges over the Spree in Berlin. The bridge used to be a border-crossing. That is why the subway line that runs over it to Warschauer Strasse was cut off when the Wall was built. During this time the subway line used to end at Schlesisches Tor.

The entire breadth of the Spree belonged to the eastern sector. This had fatal consequences for a five-year-old boy who lived in the western part in 1975. Little Cetin from Kreuzberg was playing on the river-bank when he fell into the Spree. After a few minutes West Berlin rescue service arrived, but the divers were not allowed into the water because it belonged to the heavily guarded border area. They were forced to helplessly watch as the young boy drowned. By the time the GDR border boat arrived at the scene of the accident, there was nothing

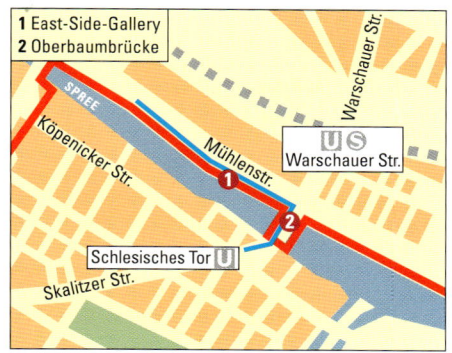

else to do but pull the dead body of the young Turkish boy out of the water.

At least the tragic death led to an agreement between West and East Berlin, which provided for mutual emergency assistance in the waters of the border area.

S-Bahn station Ostbahnhof, U- and S-Bahn station Warschauer Strasse
Time: 45 minutes

East-Side-Gallery at Mühlenstrasse (2009)

Revised and extended edition
9th Edition 2017
© 1998–2017 Jaron Verlag GmbH, Berlin
All rights reserved. This publication must not be reproduced in whole or in part without the consent of the publisher. That especially applies to reproductions, translations, micro-film and storage and processing with electronic media.
Title of the German edition: "Die Berliner Mauer".
© 1998–2017 Jaron Verlag GmbH, Berlin
Translation: Victor Dewsbery, Miriamne Fields, Richard Jay Klein
Cover design: Atelier Kattner, Berlin
Layout: Atelier Kattner, Berlin
Lithography and typography: LVD GmbH, Berlin
Maps: Edition Gauglitz, Berlin (p. 12/13) and Matthias Frach, Berlin (other maps)
Printed and bound by: Druckerei Conrad GmbH, Berlin
Printed in Germany
ISBN 978-3-89773-207-0
ISBN 978-3-89773-257-5 (5 copies)